Diversity Equity and Inclusion for Organizations

ISBN 978-976-8341-44-0

By Deborah Benjamin

Table of Contents

Understanding DEI: An Introduction

In a world rich with a mosaic of cultures, perspectives, and experiences, empathy becomes our beacon as we strive towards a more inclusive tomorrow. In the pages that follow, we seek to unravel the intricacies of diversity, equity, and inclusion (DEI)—concepts that are not only pivotal but also imperative in sculpting robust communities and thriving workplaces.

At the heart of this book lies my commitment to promoting and advancing DEI initiatives—a call to action that resonates with urgency against the backdrop of our global tapestry. We must ascend from the simple acknowledgment of diversity to the celebration and advocacy of it. Yet, the path to genuine inclusivity is often fraught with complexities and challenges that require both tenacity and grace.

Through candid stories, reflective insights, and actionable strategies, we endeavour to illuminate the multifaceted dimensions of DEI. We confront the uncomfortable truths that riddle our attempts to foster equitable spaces and strive to discern the delicate balance between acknowledging differences and championing common ground.

In a tone both empathetic and thought-provoking, this book aims to serve as a compass for those navigating the evolving landscapes of DEI—a guide to transform intentions into impactful actions. Whether you are a seasoned activist, a policy maker, company executive, or an individual seeking understanding, this book invites you to partake in a conversation that is no longer confined to the fringes but stands at the forefront of societal progress.

Join us on this exploration, as we pledge to not only lend voices to the underrepresented but also lift them in pursuit of true equity. Together, we can craft a narrative where diversity is treasured, equity is non-negotiable, and inclusion is lived. Welcome to a thoughtful expedition into the very fabric of humanity—a chronicle of striving, triumph, and the relentless pursuit of a world where every individual is valued.

The journey is long, the work is hard, but the rewards—immeasurable. Herein lies our shared manifesto for change, our blueprint for a brighter future, our bridge towards a place where everyone has the opportunity to reach their fullest potential. This is more than a book; it's a reflection, a conversation, a movement. Welcome to the pivotal dialogue on diversity, equity, and inclusion.

The History and Evolution of Diversity, Equity, and Inclusion (DEI)

In recent years, the importance of diversity, equity, and inclusion (DEI) in the workplace and society has gained significant traction. But to understand its current prominence, we must look back. The concept of DEI has evolved over time, sampling lessons from history to form the comprehensive social initiatives we see today.

Diverse Beginnings

Civil Rights and Beyond

The roots of DEI can be traced to the civil rights movements of the 1960s when efforts to end segregation and discrimination were at the forefront of American society. Framed by iconic legislation such as the Civil Rights Act of 1964 and the Voting Rights Act of 1965, this era laid the groundwork for subsequent DEI initiatives.

Affirmative Action

Out of the civil rights era arose affirmative action, a term first used by President Kennedy in 1961. Affirmative action policies aimed to provide equal opportunities in education and employment for historically marginalized groups, combating long-standing systems of oppression.

Expanding the Framework

Gender Equality Movements

The 1970s witnessed the heightening of gender equality discussions, with Title IX established to prevent sex-based discrimination in federally funded education programs. It became a legislative milestone that symbolically represented broader gender concerns within the DEI conversation.

ADA and Disability Rights

In 1990, the Americans with Disabilities Act (ADA) was enacted, providing comprehensive civil rights protection to individuals with disabilities. It solidified the notion that DEI efforts must encompass not just racial and gender diversity but also consider individuals with different abilities.

Globalization and Intersectionality

With the advent of globalization, workplaces became more diverse, and the spectrum of inclusion expanded. The introduction of intersectionality recognized that individuals don't hold just one identity but many that intersect and influence their experiences of privilege and oppression.

Modern DEI: A Holistic Approach

Today, DEI efforts consider a constellation of differences including race, ethnicity, gender, age, sexual orientation, religion, veteran status, family structure, and socioeconomic background, among others. The approach has shifted to not just tolerance or acceptance, but active celebration and advocacy.

Equity Vs. Equality

A significant evolution in thought has been the distinction between 'equity' and 'equality.' While equality means treating everyone the same, equity involves acknowledging the differing needs and conditions of individuals and providing them with resources that level the playing field.

Inclusion in Action

Inclusion has turned into action, yielding safe spaces where all voices can be heard and respected. It's about ensuring fair participation for all, creating environments where people feel confident to express their uniqueness free from judgment or disadvantage.

Technological Impact

Technology has given DEI initiatives new platforms, allowing for big data analytics to measure DEI metrics, social media to promote awareness, and AI to reduce biases in hiring processes. But, technology also brings new challenges for accessibility and the digital divide.

The Role of Social Movements

Movements like #MeToo and Black Lives Matter have shaped public discourse around DEI, challenging institutions to reexamine their cultures and policies. They stress that DEI is a continuous process—a movement, not a moment, demanding ongoing commitment and action.

DEI is an evolving philosophy, one that requires perpetual cultivation. The lessons of history inform its trajectory, and the collective effort of individuals and organizations determines its impact. Its continued focus on systemic change to reform the foundational systems and structures that maintain inequalities is a testament to humanity's capacity for growth, and a beacon for the more equitable society we strive to create.

Starting the DEI Journey: The Imperative for Organizations

We live in an era where standing for diversity, equity, and inclusion (DEI) isn't just a moral compass but a business imperative. The meticulous thread of diversity should be woven into the broader fabric of every organization, not just to check boxes or boost public image, but to genuinely cultivate an environment that embraces the unique strengths and perspectives of every individual. This isn't a mere initiative; it's the foundational shift that enterprises need to make to thrive in an increasingly globalized and interconnected world. Here's why I'm an ardent advocate for proactive and profound DEI strategies within organizations.

A Moral and Economic Case for DEI

There's an ethical argument for diversity, equity, and inclusion that's as old as humanity itself—an intrinsic belief that every individual should have an equal opportunity to contribute to society. Nevertheless, the economic and social elements are equally compelling reasons for organizations to take DEI seriously. Data consistently point to the advantage of diverse teams in terms of better problem-solving, innovation, and workplace satisfaction. McKinsey's research shows that companies in the top quartile for gender diversity are 15% more likely to outperform their peers, while those with ethnically diverse executive teams are 33% more likely to see better than average profits.

However, these statistics are merely the tip of the iceberg. Implementing DEI strategies is not only the right thing to do but one of the smartest business moves an organization can make. It has a direct impact on the bottom line, innovation, talent attraction, and retention. Furthermore, in a world population that is increasingly diverse, companies that fail to reflect this diversity risk losing relevance and their competitive edge.

The Roadmap to DEI Implementation

The crucial question then arises, how do organizations begin to implement DEI strategies? It's not a one-size-fits-all approach and requires a multifaceted plan, beginning with clear, top-down commitment from leadership. Executive buy-in is crucial; without the unwavering support of the C-suite, any attempt to foster diversity is likely to flounder.

Next, organizations must assess the current state of their DEI efforts through the lenses of recruitment, promotion, retention, and the overall workplace culture. What gets measured gets managed, and establishing key performance indicators tied to DEI goals can ensure that organizations are making visible progress.

Then comes the need to invest in the development and advancement of underrepresented talent. This can involve targeted mentorship, sponsorship programs, and a willingness to look beyond traditional pipelines to attract and retain a diverse workforce. Support structures within the organization, such as employee resource groups and affinity networks, provide a platform for underrepresented employees to voice their experiences and needs, fostering a sense of belonging and inclusion.

Lastly, organizations must constantly educate their workforce on the value of diversity and the pitfalls of bias. This should be an ongoing effort, not a one-time training session. Bias training and inclusive leadership development are just two tools in a broader toolkit of resources organizations can employ to make DEI an operational reality.

Overcoming Challenges in the Journey

The road to a truly diverse and inclusive organizational culture is paved with challenges, from confronting unconscious bias to dismantling existing power structures that perpetuate inequality. Sometimes, the challenge is simply that of unknown unknowns—organizations might not be aware of the full scope of the problem.

One major hurdle is the fear of divisiveness that some organizations associate with conversations around race, gender, and other identity facets. This is where fearless leadership and transparent, empathetic communication come into play. Creating safe spaces for dialogue, encouraging active listening, and fostering an environment where all voices are valued helps bridge these divides.

Another common obstacle is the inertia of **the way things have always been done**. Change, particularly in large, established organizations, can be slow and met with resistance. Here, it's vital to articulate the business case for change, using both qualitative and quantitative data to show how DEI is not just a moral mandate but a strategic imperative.

The Ripple Effect of Inclusive Cultures

The beauty of fostering a truly inclusive organizational culture lies in its ripple effect. When employees feel that they can bring their whole, authentic selves to work, there's a positive impact on morale, creativity, and ultimately, the ability of the organization to innovate. This translates into a better customer experience, as the diversity of employees mirrors that of the customer base, leading to more relatable products and services.

A key benefit is the ability to attract and retain top talent. Younger generations, in particular, are placing a high value on working for organizations that share their values, and a company with a robust DEI strategy is far more likely to be seen as a desirable employer.

Lastly, an inclusive culture is part of an ongoing commitment to corporate social responsibility. It's an opportunity for an organization to be a force for good in the broader community, contributing to a more equitable society where everyone has an opportunity to succeed.

A Call to Action

The statistics and arguments in favour of DEI are compelling, but the strongest incentive comes from the simple fact that it's the right thing to do. High-performing organizations of the future will be those that recognize and celebrate the unique strengths of their people.

We're not talking about a superficial nod to diversity in a corporate brochure; we're talking about a fundamental, operational shift in how organizations think about their people, their products, and their purpose in the world. The imperative to begin that shift is now, not just because it's economically sound, but because it's a reflection of the kind of world we all want to live in.

The resistance to change may be strong, but the resolve to see it through is stronger. It's time for organizations to roll up their sleeves and get to work on achieving the DEI vision that's not just good for business, but good for the world. Let's start the journey together. #Diversity #Equity #Inclusion #DEIImplementation #CorporateResponsibility.

Defining Diversity in the Modern Workplace

In today's global economy, **diversity** in the workplace extends beyond the conventional parameters of race and gender. It encapsulates a broad spectrum of attributes and experiences such as ethnicity, sexual orientation, age, religious beliefs, physical abilities, as well as socio-economic status, education, and cultural background. Diversity is about recognizing and valuing the unique perspectives and life experiences each individual brings to an organization.

In a modern workplace setting, diversity means creating an inclusive environment that respects and integrates individual differences, offering equal opportunities for all employees. This environment supports a culture of openness, mutual respect, and cooperation, aiming to combine different talents and insights to foster innovation and creativity. Here is a closer look at the multiple dimensions of diversity:

Cultural and Ethnic Diversity

Cultural and ethnic diversity refers to the variety of cultural traditions, languages, and experiences individuals bring to the workforce. An inclusive workplace respects these differences and leverages them to create a richer work environment.

Gender and Sexual Orientation

Workplaces are moving toward a more balanced representation across all gender identities and sexual orientations, creating equitable opportunities for career progression and expression without discrimination.

Age Diversity

Incorporating a range of ages within a team can bring together the wisdom and experience of older employees with the fresh perspectives of younger ones, promoting an intergenerational exchange of ideas.

Religious and Spiritual Beliefs

The acknowledgment of varying religious and spiritual beliefs within a workforce ensures that employees feel respected and accommodated for, which may include time for religious practices and flexible holiday schedules.

Physical and Mental Abilities

Creating an accessible workplace that is accommodating to individuals with different physical and mental abilities is essential. This not only pertains to physical office layout but also to the tools, technologies, and resources provided.

Socio-economic and Educational Diversity

Diversity includes the variety of life experiences shaped by socio-economic backgrounds and educational levels, which contribute to a workforce equipped with a wide array of skills, insights, and problem-solving abilities.

Neurodiversity

Recognizing and valuing neurodiversity acknowledges the strengths of individuals with neurocognitive differences, such as autism spectrum disorder, ADHD, and others, and provides support systems to allow them to excel in their roles.

A truly diverse workplace reflects the society in which it operates and draws from the widest possible pool of talent. It recognizes that when people from different backgrounds and with different points of view work together, they can solve problems, create innovative solutions, and drive business success in a way that homogeneous environments seldom do.

In the contemporary context, diversity is often delivered in conjunction with equality and inclusion to ensure not just a mix of people but also an atmosphere where all individuals have a sense of belonging, equity, and voice in the workforce.

Equity vs. Equality: Knowing the Difference

In discussions of social justice, the terms equity and equality are often used interchangeably. However, they refer to distinct concepts that approach fairness and justice from different angles. Understanding the difference between equity and equality is essential for effectively addressing the unique challenges faced by diverse groups within society.

What is Equality?

Equality is about providing the same level of opportunity and assistance to all segments of society. In theory, this approach treats everyone the same regardless of their starting point or the barriers they face. An equal approach assumes that everyone benefits from the same supports. It is built on the assumption that fairness is achieved when everyone is treated identically.

An everyday example of equality in action would be giving every student the same textbook. It's equal because every student has the same resource. However, it doesn't take into account whether or not the textbook is accessible to everyone based on language, learning ability, or whether the content is culturally relevant or not.

What is Equity?

Equity, on the other hand, is about fairness. It's an approach that ensures everyone has access to the same opportunities. Equity recognizes that advantages and barriers—the proverbial "playing field"—are not the same for everyone and, therefore, different people need different resources and opportunities to reach an equal outcome.

For instance, in the case of the students, equity would mean providing additional resources to students who may not speak English as a first language or who have learning disabilities so they can fully understand the material.

Equity aims to identify and eliminate barriers that prevent the full participation of some groups. To promote equity, policies and procedures may need to be modified to accommodate differences resulting from historical disadvantages or inequality.

Equity vs. Equality in Different Contexts

Education

In education, equality means giving every student the same resources; equity means distributing resources based on the needs of the students. An equitable educational environment understands that some children come from disadvantaged backgrounds and need additional support to have the same potential for success as others.

Healthcare

Equality in healthcare would mean providing every patient with the same type of care, while equity involves customizing care to reflect each patient's unique health circumstances. This often means giving more attention to those who start with poorer health.

Workplace

In the workplace, equality might involve giving all employees the same compensation and opportunities. However, equity would ensure that there is fairness in hiring practices, promotions, and compensation that acknowledges and addresses factors like gender, race, and other socioeconomic factors.

Why Does the Difference Matter?

Understanding the distinction between equity and equality is vital to creating a society that is truly fair and just. When we aim merely for equality, we assume that the playing field is level, and that's often not the case. Equity speaks to a deeper level of fairness that seeks to provide everyone with what they need to be successful.

The pursuit of equity acknowledges unequal starting places and seeks to correct the imbalance. Policies and practices that factor in equity can create an environment where everyone has the tools they need to succeed and participate fully in society.

While related, equity and equality are not the same. Equality aims to promote fairness by treating everyone the same despite their differences, which can ultimately maintain and exacerbate disparity. Equity, in striving for fairness, seeks to understand individual circumstances and provide the necessary resources and opportunities for an equal outcome.

It's not a matter of which concept is better but rather understanding when and how to apply them. While equality is the ultimate goal, equity is the means to get there. By focusing on equity, we can build the pathways for all individuals to reach the destination of equality, regardless of where their journey started.

Knowing the difference between these two concepts is not just an exercise in vocabulary—it's about recognizing that true inclusion and fairness are about more than surface-level assessments. It's about digging deeper to uplift those who are at a disadvantage so that everyone has a fair shot at success.

Building Equitable Systems for Opportunity and Growth in the Context of DEI

In recent years, conversations surrounding diversity, equity, and inclusion (DEI) have gained significant momentum across various sectors of society. From corporate boardrooms to educational institutions, the necessity of creating equitable systems that foster opportunity and growth has become a focal point. Equity goes beyond the surface-level diversity metrics and aims at dismantling systemic barriers that hinder equal opportunities. This essay explores the importance of building equitable systems in the context of DEI and how such systems can catalyze opportunity and growth.

Understanding Equity in DEI

Equity is often conflated with equality, but the two concepts are distinct. While equality involves treating everyone the same, equity recognizes that individuals come from different starting points and may require different resources and opportunities to achieve similar outcomes. In the context of DEI, equity means creating systems that provide fair access to resources, opportunities, and support for all individuals, regardless of their race, gender, socioeconomic status, or other identity markers.

The Importance of Equitable Systems

1. Promoting Fairness and Justice

At its core, equity is about fairness and justice. An equitable system acknowledges historical and structural inequalities and actively works to redress them. This is particularly important in areas like education, employment, and healthcare, where systemic biases have long perpetuated disparities. By ensuring that all individuals have access to the resources and opportunities they need to succeed, equitable systems promote a more just and fair society.

2. Enhancing Organizational Performance

Research consistently shows that diverse and inclusive organizations outperform their less inclusive counterparts. However, diversity alone is not enough. Without equitable systems, diverse teams may not reach their full potential. Equitable systems ensure that all team members have the support and opportunities they need to contribute meaningfully, fostering an environment where diverse perspectives can thrive. This leads to increased creativity, innovation, and problem-solving capabilities, enhancing overall organizational performance.

3. Fostering Economic Growth

Equitable systems are also crucial for broader economic growth. When individuals are given fair access to opportunities, they are more likely to reach their full potential and contribute to the economy. This is particularly important for marginalized communities, who have historically been excluded from many economic opportunities. By investing in equitable systems, we can unlock the potential of all individuals, driving innovation, entrepreneurship, and economic development.

Building Equitable Systems: Key Strategies

1. Addressing Systemic Barriers

To build equitable systems, it is essential to identify and address systemic barriers that hinder equal opportunities. This requires a thorough examination of existing policies, practices, and structures to uncover biases and disparities. For example, in the workplace, this might involve analyzing hiring and promotion practices to ensure they are free from bias and provide equal opportunities for all employees.

2. Implementing Inclusive Policies

Inclusive policies are foundational to building equitable systems. These policies should be designed to provide fair access to resources and opportunities for all individuals. This might include implementing flexible work arrangements to accommodate diverse needs, providing targeted support and mentorship programs for underrepresented groups, and ensuring equal pay for equal work.

3. Fostering a Culture of Inclusion

Building an equitable system requires more than just policy changes; it also requires a cultural shift. Organizations must foster a culture of inclusion where all individuals feel valued and respected. This involves promoting awareness and understanding of DEI issues, encouraging open and honest conversations, and holding leaders accountable for creating inclusive environments.

4. Measuring and Monitoring Progress

To ensure that efforts to build equitable systems are effective, it is crucial to measure and monitor progress. This involves collecting and analyzing data on key DEI metrics, such as representation, pay equity, and employee engagement. Regularly assessing progress allows organizations to identify areas for improvement and make data-driven decisions to advance equity.

Building equitable systems for opportunity and growth is not only a moral imperative but also a strategic necessity in today's diverse and interconnected world. By addressing systemic barriers, implementing inclusive policies, fostering a culture of inclusion, and measuring progress, we can create environments where all individuals have the opportunity to thrive. In doing so, we promote fairness and justice, enhance organizational performance, and drive broader economic growth. As we continue to advance DEI efforts, let us commit to building equitable systems that pave the way for a more inclusive and prosperous future for all.

The Pillars of Inclusion and Belonging

In today's diverse global landscape, the concepts of inclusion and belonging have become central tenets for organizations and communities worldwide. As we strive to build more equitable and supportive environments, understanding the foundational pillars of inclusion and belonging is paramount. In this article, we will explore these core principles and discuss why they matter in fostering cultures where everyone feels valued and empowered to contribute their best.

Representational Diversity

One of the first pillars of inclusion is representational diversity. This means that an organization or community includes people from a wide range of backgrounds, including different races, ethnicities, genders, sexual orientations, age groups, and abilities. Diversity isn't just about numbers; it is about valuing variety in experiences and perspectives that can enhance creativity and drive innovation.

Equitable Opportunities

Inclusion cannot exist without equity. Equitable opportunities mean all individuals have fair access to resources and possibilities for growth such as education, job promotions, or community involvement. Equity levels the playing field, so to speak, by recognizing and addressing barriers that might prevent certain groups from fully participating or succeeding.

Inclusive Policies and Practices

Policies and practices are the backbone of inclusive environments. This pillar involves creating and implementing guidelines that support diverse needs. This might include offering flexible work arrangements, ensuring accessibility for people with disabilities, providing inclusive healthcare benefits, or developing anti-discrimination protocols.

Awareness and Education

To build inclusive spaces, there must be a commitment to ongoing awareness and education. This involves regular training on topics such as unconscious bias, microaggressions, cultural competence, and allyship. Education not only enlightens but also empowers individuals to recognize and challenge biases and inequities that may exist within themselves and their environments.

Supportive Leadership

Leadership plays a crucial role in fostering inclusion and belonging. Supportive leadership is not just about endorsing diversity initiatives but also about leaders actively demonstrating inclusive behavior, advocating for underrepresented voices, and holding others accountable for creating an inclusive culture.

Open Communication

Open, honest communication is vital for inclusion. It helps build trust and allows individuals to express concerns and contribute ideas without fear of repercussion. A culture of open communication is one where feedback is encouraged and used constructively to improve personal interactions and organizational policies.

Sense of Belonging

Ultimately, the goal of inclusion practices is to cultivate a sense of belonging – a feeling that one's presence and contributions are welcome and important. To foster belonging, spaces must not only be physically accessible but also psychologically supportive, where each person feels recognized, respected, and connected to the community.

Measurable Actions and Accountability

Lastly, inclusion efforts must be paired with measurable actions and accountability. This means setting specific, objective goals for improving inclusion, regularly assessing progress, and being transparent about the outcomes. Without metrics and accountability, inclusion initiatives can easily become empty promises devoid of real impact.

The pillars of inclusion and belonging are interdependent; each supports and reinforces the others. By focusing on these principles, organizations and communities can move beyond superficial efforts to create environments where diversity thrives, and every individual can feel truly included and valued. It is an ongoing endeavor that requires commitment from everyone involved. Together, we can dismantle barriers and build a world characterized by unity in diversity.

Diversity, Equity, and Inclusion (DEI) in Recruitment, Retention, and Development

In today's globally interconnected and culturally diverse world, the importance of diversity, equity, and inclusion (DEI) in organizational practices cannot be overstated. The workforce is evolving rapidly, and businesses must adapt to ensure they are attracting, retaining, and developing talent from all backgrounds. DEI is not just a moral imperative but a business necessity that drives innovation, improves decision-making, and enhances company reputation. This essay explores DEI in the realms of recruitment, retention, and development within the Human Resources (HR) landscape.

DEI in Recruitment

Inclusive Job Descriptions

The recruitment process begins with job descriptions. It is essential to craft job postings that are inclusive and free from gender-biased language or other forms of discriminatory phrasing. Tools and resources, such as gender decoder software, can help identify and correct biases in job descriptions.

Diverse Talent Pools

To attract a diverse range of candidates, organizations must reach out to varied talent pools. This includes posting job openings on platforms that cater to underrepresented groups, partnering with minority-focused professional organizations, and attending diversity job fairs. By widening the net, companies can ensure they are considering candidates from all walks of life.

Unbiased Screening Processes

Implementing blind recruitment techniques can significantly reduce unconscious bias. This might involve removing names, ages, and other identifying information from resumes during the initial screening process. Additionally, utilizing AI-driven applicant tracking systems (ATS) can help ensure candidates are judged solely on their qualifications and experience.

Diverse Interview Panels

Having a diverse interview panel is crucial in mitigating bias and ensuring a fair evaluation of candidates. Such panels bring varied perspectives and can help identify the best candidate based on merit rather than similarity to existing staff. Training interviewers in unconscious bias can further enhance the fairness of the recruitment process.

DEI in Retention

Employee Resource Groups (ERGs)

ERGs play a vital role in fostering a sense of belonging among employees. These groups, often formed around shared characteristics such as race, gender, or sexual orientation, provide support, networking opportunities, and a platform for voicing concerns. Encouraging and supporting the formation of ERGs can help retain diverse talent by creating an inclusive workplace culture.

Equitable Policies and Practices

Equity in the workplace means ensuring all employees have access to the same opportunities and resources. This involves scrutinizing company policies and practices to remove systemic barriers that might disadvantage certain groups. Examples include equitable parental leave policies, flexible working arrangements, and fair performance evaluation processes.

Continuous Feedback and Improvement

Regularly soliciting feedback from employees about their experiences can provide invaluable insights into the effectiveness of DEI initiatives. Surveys, focus groups, and one-on-one meetings can help identify areas for improvement and ensure that all employees feel heard and valued. Acting on this feedback demonstrates a commitment to continuous improvement and can enhance employee satisfaction and retention.

DEI in Development

Inclusive Training Programs

Development opportunities must be accessible to all employees, regardless of their background. This includes offering diverse training programs that cater to various learning styles and providing support for employees with disabilities. Additionally, leadership development programs should specifically target underrepresented groups to ensure a diverse pipeline of future leaders.

Mentorship and Sponsorship

Mentorship programs can play a significant role in career development, particularly for employees from underrepresented groups. Pairing these employees with mentors who can offer guidance, support, and networking opportunities can help them navigate their career paths effectively. Sponsorship goes a step further, with senior leaders advocating for the advancement of high-potential employees from diverse backgrounds.

Career Pathways and Advancement

Organizations must ensure that there are clear and equitable pathways for career advancement. This involves transparently communicating promotion criteria, providing regular performance feedback, and offering development opportunities that prepare employees for higher-level roles. Ensuring that all employees have access to these opportunities is crucial for fostering an inclusive environment where everyone can thrive.

Diversity, equity, and inclusion in recruitment, retention, and development are critical components of any successful organization. By implementing inclusive recruitment practices, fostering an equitable workplace culture, and providing development opportunities for all employees, businesses can not only attract and retain top talent but also drive innovation, improve decision-making, and enhance their overall performance. Embracing DEI is not just a strategic advantage but a reflection of a company's commitment to creating a fair and inclusive society.

Communicating DEI: Language, Dialogue, and Policies

In recent years, Diversity, Equity, and Inclusion (DEI) have become essential components of organizational culture. As workplaces become increasingly diverse, the importance of effectively communicating DEI principles cannot be overstated. This essay explores the critical aspects of communicating DEI, focusing on the roles of language, dialogue, and policies in fostering an inclusive environment.

The Power of Language in DEI Communication

Language is a powerful tool in shaping perceptions and fostering inclusivity. The words we choose and the way we communicate can either build bridges or create barriers. In the context of DEI, using inclusive language is fundamental. Inclusive language involves deliberately selecting words that respect and acknowledge the diversity of individuals and groups.

Gender-Inclusive Language

Using gender-neutral terms is one way to ensure that language is inclusive. For example, using "they/them" pronouns instead of assuming "he/him" or "she/her" can make a significant difference in making non-binary and genderqueer individuals feel recognized and respected. Additionally, replacing terms like "chairman" with "chairperson" or "fireman" with "firefighter" helps to avoid gender bias.

Culturally Sensitive Language

Being culturally sensitive in our language choices also plays a crucial role in DEI communication. This involves acknowledging and respecting different cultural backgrounds and avoiding language that could be perceived as offensive or dismissive. For instance, being mindful of the preferred terms for ethnic and racial groups, and avoiding stereotypes, contributes to a more inclusive environment.

Dialogue: Creating Open and Honest Conversations

Dialogue is another key element in communicating DEI effectively. Open and honest conversations about diversity, equity, and inclusion help in breaking down barriers and building understanding among employees. However, fostering such dialogue requires a strategic approach.

Creating Safe Spaces

Creating safe spaces where individuals feel comfortable sharing their experiences and perspectives is vital. Safe spaces are environments free from judgment, where employees can speak openly without fear of retaliation. Organizations can facilitate these spaces by establishing clear ground rules and ensuring that all participants are committed to respectful and constructive dialogue.

Active Listening

Active listening is an essential skill in DEI conversations. It involves genuinely listening to others, understanding their perspectives, and responding thoughtfully. Active listening not only validates the experiences of marginalized individuals but also helps in identifying areas where the organization can improve its DEI efforts.

Facilitating Difficult Conversations

DEI conversations can sometimes be challenging, as they may involve addressing sensitive issues such as discrimination, privilege, and bias. Skilled facilitators who can navigate these discussions with empathy and impartiality are invaluable. They can help mediate conflicts, encourage participation, and ensure that all voices are heard.

Policies: Institutionalizing DEI

While language and dialogue are crucial, institutionalizing DEI through concrete policies is equally important. Policies provide a framework for consistent and equitable practices within an organization. They signal a commitment to DEI and hold the organization accountable for its actions.

Anti-Discrimination Policies

Anti-discrimination policies are foundational to any DEI strategy. These policies should clearly define what constitutes discriminatory behavior and outline the procedures for reporting and addressing such behavior. They should cover various aspects of identity, including race, gender, sexual orientation, disability, and religion, among others.

Recruitment and Hiring Practices

Inclusive recruitment and hiring practices are essential for creating a diverse workforce. Organizations should aim to eliminate biases in their hiring processes by implementing practices such as blind recruitment, diverse hiring panels, and standardized interview questions. Additionally, setting diversity targets and regularly reviewing hiring data can help ensure that the organization is making progress toward its DEI goals.

Training and Development

Ongoing training and development programs focused on DEI are critical for fostering an inclusive culture. These programs should cover topics such as unconscious bias, cultural competency, and inclusive leadership. Providing employees with the knowledge and skills to navigate diversity is key to creating an environment where everyone feels valued and respected.

Accountability Mechanisms

To ensure that DEI policies are effective, organizations must establish accountability mechanisms. This could involve regular audits of DEI practices, employee surveys to gauge the inclusiveness of the workplace, and transparent reporting on DEI metrics. Holding leadership accountable for DEI progress through performance reviews and tying DEI outcomes to executive compensation can also drive meaningful change.

Communicating DEI effectively requires a multifaceted approach that encompasses inclusive language, open dialogue, and robust policies. By paying attention to the words we use, fostering honest conversations, and institutionalizing DEI through concrete policies, organizations can create inclusive environments where diversity is not only acknowledged but celebrated. As we move forward, a continued commitment to DEI communication will be essential in building equitable and inclusive workplaces for all.

Cultivating a Diverse Workforce: Strategies and Best Practices

Introduction to Diversity in the Workplace

In today's global economy, diversity in the workforce is more than a buzzword; it's an integral component of a successful business strategy. A diverse workforce brings a plethora of perspectives, experiences, and skills to the table, enabling companies to be more creative, adaptable, and competitive. This article will explore the importance of diversity, the benefits it offers, and the strategies and best practices for cultivating a diverse workforce.

The Importance of Workforce Diversity

Workforce diversity goes beyond hiring individuals from various racial, gender, and ethnic backgrounds. It encompasses age, sexual orientation, religious beliefs, disability, and socioeconomic status, among others. By fostering an inclusive environment where all these differences are valued, businesses can tap into a wide range of talents and insights that would otherwise be inaccessible.

Benefits of a Diverse Workforce

1. **Enhanced Creativity and Innovation**: Diverse teams are proven to be more creative and innovative. Different backgrounds mean different approaches to problem-solving and a wider array of ideas.

2. **Increased Market Reach**: A diverse workforce reflects a diverse market. Employees can provide insights into different customer segments, leading to better-targeted products and services.

3. **Improved Employee Performance**: Inclusive companies often report higher job satisfaction among their staff, which can lead to higher productivity and reduced employee turnover.

4. **Better Decision-Making**: Diverse teams make better decisions faster, as they consider a wider range of perspectives, leading to improved business performance.

5. **Enhanced Company Reputation**: Prioritizing diversity can improve a company's reputation, making it more attractive to top talent and customers who value social responsibility.

Strategies for Cultivating Diversity

1. **Commitment from Leadership**: A meaningful commitment to diversity must start at the top. Leaders should set clear goals for diversity and inclusion, and hold themselves accountable for reaching them.

2. **Bias-Free Recruitment**: Implement recruitment strategies that mitigate unconscious bias. This might include structured interviews, diverse hiring panels, and blind resume reviews.

3. **Diversity Training**: Invest in regular training to help employees and management understand the importance of di-

versity and how to foster an inclusive environment.

4. **Mentorship Programs**: These programs can help underrepresented groups within the company gain the experience and confidence necessary to climb the corporate ladder.

5. **Create Employee Resource Groups (ERGs)**: ERGs are volunteer groups that provide support, advocacy, and education, centered around particular groups such as LGBTQ employees or veterans.

6. **Inclusive Culture**: Create a culture where all employees feel welcomed and valued. This can include policies and practices that accommodate different cultures and lifestyles.

Best Practices for Maintaining Diversity

1. **Continuous Assessment**: Regularly assess diversity goals and metrics to ensure that your strategies are effective and to identify areas for improvement.

2. **Open Communication**: Foster an environment where employees feel comfortable discussing diversity and inclusion. Open dialogues can help surface issues that might not otherwise come to light.

3. **Encouraging Employee Participation**: Give employees a voice in diversity initiatives and the decision-making process. This involvement can increase engagement and buy-in.

4. **Integration into Company Values**: Diversity should be integrated into the core values of the company, reflected in its mission, operations, and business practices.

5. **Addressing Discrimination Promptly**: Have a zero-tolerance policy for discrimination and ensure that all complaints are taken seriously and handled promptly and effectively.

Cultivating a diverse workforce is not a one-off initiative but a continuous effort that requires dedication, commitment, and strategic action. By implementing these strategies and best practices, companies can build a workforce that embodies a range of experiences and perspectives, driving innovation and reflecting the diversity of the global marketplace. In doing so, they not only enhance their performance but also contribute positively to a more inclusive and equitable society.

Businesses and HR professionals looking for more information on implementing diversity programs can consult these resources to get started or improve their existing efforts. Remember, the pursuit of diversity and inclusion is a journey that evolves with society and your own workforce, requiring an adaptable and ongoing approach.

Addressing Bias and Discrimination: Tools for Change

In today's increasingly globalized world, the issues of bias and discrimination remain pervasive, affecting individuals and communities across various dimensions of society. From workplaces to educational institutions, and even within cultural and social settings, these prejudices create barriers to equality and justice. Addressing bias and discrimination is not only a moral imperative but also crucial for fostering inclusive environments that allow for the full participation and potential of all individuals. This essay explores the tools and strategies that can be employed to combat these issues effectively.

Understanding Bias and Discrimination

Before delving into the tools for change, it is essential to understand what bias and discrimination entail. Bias refers to a predisposition or preconceived notion about individuals or groups, often rooted in stereotypes. These biases can be explicit (conscious) or implicit (unconscious). Discrimination, on the other hand, involves actions or behaviors that treat people unfairly based on characteristics such as race, gender, age, sexual orientation, religion, or disability.

Tools for Change

Education and Awareness

One of the most powerful tools for addressing bias and discrimination is education. Raising awareness about the existence and impact of these issues can lead to greater empathy and understanding. Educational programs should include:

- **Bias Training**: Programs that help individuals recognize their implicit biases and understand how these biases influence their behavior.

- **Diversity and Inclusion Workshops**: Sessions that educate participants about the importance of diversity and inclusion, and provide strategies for creating more inclusive environments.

- **Cultural Competency**: Training that enhances individuals' ability to interact effectively with people from different cultural backgrounds.

Policy and Legislation

Effective policies and legislation are crucial for addressing systemic discrimination. Governments and organizations must implement and enforce laws that protect individuals from discriminatory practices. Important legislative tools include:

- **Anti-Discrimination Laws**: Legal frameworks that prohibit discrimination based on race, gender, age, disability, and other protected characteristics.

- **Equal Employment Opportunity Policies**: Regulations that ensure fair hiring, promotion, and compensation practices within organizations.

- **Affirmative Action**: Policies that aim to correct historical injustices and provide opportunities for marginalized groups.

Advocacy and Activism

Advocacy and activism play critical roles in driving social change. By raising their voices, individuals and groups can bring attention to issues of bias and discrimination and push for necessary reforms. Key strategies include:

- **Grassroots Movements**: Community-based efforts to raise awareness and demand change.

- **Public Campaigns**: Initiatives that use media and public platforms to highlight discrimination and advocate for equality.

- **Alliances and Coalitions**: Partnerships between various organizations and groups to amplify their impact and reach.

Organizational Change

Organizations must take proactive steps to address bias and discrimination within their structures. This involves:

- **Inclusive Hiring Practices**: Ensuring diverse representation in hiring processes and decision-making roles.

- **Bias-Free Performance Reviews**: Implementing evaluation systems that minimize personal biases and focus on objective criteria.

- **Employee Resource Groups (ERGs)**: Providing support networks for employees from marginalized groups.

Technological Solutions

In the digital age, technology can be leveraged to combat bias and discrimination. Examples include:

- **Bias Detection Software**: Tools that analyze language and behavior for signs of bias, helping organizations identify and address issues.

- **Anonymized Recruitment**: Platforms that remove identifying information from resumes and applications to reduce bias in hiring.

- **Online Training Modules**: Interactive and accessible training programs that educate individuals about bias and discrimination.

Addressing bias and discrimination is a multifaceted challenge that requires a comprehensive and sustained effort. By employing tools such as education, policy and legislation, advocacy, organizational change, and technological solutions, society can make significant strides toward equality and justice. It is the collective responsibility of individuals, organizations, and governments to work together to dismantle the barriers of prejudice and create inclusive environments where everyone has the opportunity to thrive. Through continued commitment and action, we can move closer to a world free from bias and discrimination.

Metrics That Matter: Measuring DEI Progress

Diversity, Equity, and Inclusion (DEI) have become critical components of organizational success in the modern business landscape. Organizations worldwide are increasingly recognizing the value that diverse perspectives bring to innovation, decision-making, and overall performance. However, moving beyond intention to meaningful action requires more than just initiatives and policies—it necessitates the ability to measure progress effectively. This essay explores the essential metrics for assessing DEI progress and how these metrics can help organizations create a more inclusive and equitable workplace.

The Importance of Measuring DEI

Before diving into specific metrics, it is crucial to understand why measuring DEI is important. Metrics provide a concrete way to assess the effectiveness of DEI initiatives, identify areas for improvement, and hold the organization accountable for its commitments. Without measurement, DEI efforts risk becoming superficial gestures rather than driving substantive change.

Metrics also help in:

1. **Benchmarking Progress**: Establishing a baseline and tracking changes over time.

2. **Evaluating Impact**: Determining whether DEI initiatives are achieving their intended outcomes.

3. **Informed Decision-Making**: Providing data-driven insights to guide policy and strategy adjustments.

4. **Transparency and Accountability**: Demonstrating commitment to stakeholders, including employees, investors, and customers.

Key Metrics for Measuring DEI Progress

While there is no one-size-fits-all approach to measuring DEI, certain metrics have emerged as particularly valuable. These metrics can be broadly categorized into quantitative and qualitative measures.

Quantitative Metrics

1. **Representation Metrics**

- **Workforce Demographics**: Analyzing the composition of the workforce across various dimensions such as race, gender, age, disability status, and more. This includes examining representation at different levels of the organization, from entry-level positions to executive roles.

- **Hiring and Promotion Rates**: Tracking the rates at which diverse candidates are hired and promoted compared to their non-diverse counterparts. This helps identify potential biases in recruitment and advancement processes.

2. **Pay Equity**

- **Salary Comparisons**: Comparing compensation across different demographic groups to identify and address pay disparities. This can include analyzing base salary, bonuses, and other forms of compensation.

- **Pay Gap Analysis**: Conducting regular pay gap analyses to uncover structural inequities and ensure fair compensation practices.

3. **Retention and Turnover Rates**

- **Attrition Rates**: Monitoring the turnover rates of diverse employees compared to their peers. High attrition rates among specific groups can indicate issues with workplace culture or inclusivity.

- **Tenure Analysis**: Examining the length of time employees from diverse backgrounds stay with the organization, providing insights into their experiences and satisfaction.

Qualitative Metrics

1. **Employee Engagement and Satisfaction**

- **Surveys and Feedback**: Conducting regular surveys to gauge employee perceptions of the organization's DEI efforts. Questions can cover areas such as inclusivity, sense of belonging, and perceptions of fairness.

- **Focus Groups and Interviews**: Facilitating focus groups and one-on-one interviews to gather in-depth insights into employees' experiences and identify areas for improvement.

2. **Inclusion Index**

- **Climate Assessments**: Developing an inclusion index based on factors such as psychological safety, respect, and access to opportunities. This can be derived from survey responses and direct feedback.

- **Belonging Scores**: Measuring employees' sense of belonging within the organization and their perception of how well their unique perspectives are valued.

3. **Leadership Accountability**

- **DEI Goals and KPIs**: Setting specific DEI goals and key performance indicators (KPIs) for leaders and holding them accountable for progress. This can include goals related to representation, pay equity, and inclusion initiatives.

- **Leadership Commitment**: Assessing the extent to which leaders actively champion and participate in DEI efforts, including their participation in training and advocacy.

Implementing DEI Metrics Effectively

To make the most of these metrics, organizations need a strategic approach to implementation. Here are some best practices:

1. **Define Clear Objectives**: Establish clear and measurable DEI objectives aligned with the organization's overall mission and values.

2. **Ensure Data Accuracy**: Collect and analyze data accurately, respecting employee privacy and adhering to ethical standards.

3. **Regular Reporting**: Create regular reports to track progress and share findings with stakeholders. Transparency is key to building trust and accountability.

4. **Continuous Improvement**: Use the insights gained from metrics to continuously refine and improve DEI initiatives. This includes being open to feedback and willing to make necessary changes.

5. **Engage Employees**: Involve employees in the process by soliciting their input and keeping them informed about DEI efforts and outcomes.

Measuring DEI progress is not just about ticking boxes—it is about fostering a culture of accountability, transparency, and continuous improvement. By focusing on both quantitative and qualitative metrics, organizations can gain a comprehensive understanding of their DEI landscape and make informed decisions that drive meaningful change. Ultimately, the goal is to create a workplace where diversity is celebrated, equity is ensured, and inclusion is a lived experience for all employees.

The Economics of Inclusion: The Business Case for DEI

In the wake of cultural transformation and a critical look at corporate practices, diversity, equity, and inclusion (DEI) have ascended from mere buzzwords to the very fabric of corporate discourse. Corporations are increasingly being called upon to adopt an equity minded approach to their operations, not just as a moral obligation but also as a business imperative. It is no longer enough for companies to simply tout diversity; they must embed these principles into every aspect of their business, from hiring and promotion to product development and customer service.

In the cutthroat world of business, diversity, equity, and inclusion (DEI) might seem like buzzwords that get thrown around as part of corporate jargon, often without a true understanding or commitment. Yet, those who dismiss DEI as a passing trend do so at their peril. I am an advocate of DEI, not because it's the 'right' thing to do, but because it's an essential driver of sustainable business growth, innovation, and long-term viability. The question then becomes not "if," but "how" to incorporate DEI into the core DNA of businesses.

Innovation Through Diverse Perspectives

Beyond the compelling moral narrative, there exists an equally persuasive economic argument. A McKinsey analysis found that companies in the top quartile for ethnic and cultural diversity in management were 33% more likely to have industry-leading profitability. Additionally, data published in the Harvard Business Review illustrates a positive correlation between diverse leadership and financial outperformance.

These findings underscore that diversity, when accompanied by inclusion and equity, is not a mere box to check but an active ingredient in driving a company's success. The DNA of innovation is diversity. Homogenous teams think in lockstep and often find themselves hitting a creative wall. Conversely, diverse teams naturally bring a variety of life experiences, worldviews, and problem-solving approaches to the table, sparking the innovative thinking that businesses need to stay ahead. Studies consistently show that diverse companies are more innovative and perform better financially.

The Consumer Connection

The modern-day consumer is more informed, discerning, and values-driven than their predecessors. They're more likely to patronize companies that reflect their beliefs and values, and are quick to shun those who don't.

Incorporating DEI into business processes is not about meeting quotas or appearances. It is about fostering an inclusive work environment, where each employee feels valued and can reach their full potential. Companies that succeed in this objective often create more innovation, higher-performing teams, and a greater competitive edge. The integration of diverse perspectives encourages more comprehensive problem-solving approaches, leading to broader market appeal and innovative product lines. A DEI framework doesn't just foster an inclusive workplace; it also ensures that businesses can better understand and connect with an increasingly diverse customer base.

Attracting and Retaining Talent

Employees want to work for companies that not only tolerate but celebrate their differences. In a competitive job market, a commitment to DEI can be the differentiating factor in attracting top talent. It's equally important in retaining employees; those who feel valued and heard are more likely to stay and contribute to their full potential. This seismic shift is demanding more than just lip service; it requires concrete actions that necessitate a reevaluation of culture, policies, and procedures, from hiring and compensation to career development and resource allocation. It requires companies to ask some tough questions, such as "Does our recruitment process inadvertently favor certain demographics?" or "Do our benefits and policies accommodate a diverse range of needs?"

The transformation toward DEI should be seen as an iterative process, one that necessitates continual reassessment and adaptation.

Mitigating Risk and Anticipating Changes

The world is changing, and so are the laws and regulations that govern businesses. Organizations that fail to prioritize DEI leave themselves open to legal, reputational, and operational risks. By proactively addressing these issues, companies can build more sustainable and resilient business models.

The Call to Action

Implementing DEI is not just an HR checklist item — it's a strategic business imperative. The true litmus test for a company's dedication to DEI is whether these principles are enshrined in daily operations and decision-making. From language use in company materials to the communication norms in meetings, there should be a conscious effort to create an environment that reflects and respects the diversity within the organization. This operationalization of equity sends a powerful message to employees, partners, and customers about the core values of the company.

Corporate leaders must champion this cause, not only because it is ethically sound but because it makes economic sense. Leadership must take a proactive role in championing diversity by not only advocating for DEI policies but also embodying those values in their actions. This means holding themselves and their teams accountable for fostering inclusive practices. Transparent communication and setting clear goals are vital in this effort. Leaders should also strive to create an open dialogue about DEI, ensuring that it is part of the company's narrative and that everyone feels a stake in advancing these principles.

In a world where the only constant is change, businesses must adapt or become obsolete. DEI is not just a tool for adaptation; it's a blueprint for a prosperous, inclusive, and sustainable future. In doing so, businesses will discover new pathways to innovation, growth, and lasting value. This is the anthem that businesses should be singing—not as an obligation, but as an opportunity.

Legal Frameworks Shaping DEI Efforts: A Comprehensive Analysis

Diversity, Equity, and Inclusion (DEI) have become central tenets in the mission statements of organizations across the globe. While these principles promote ethical motivations towards creating inclusive environments, they are also heavily influenced and regulated by a variety of legal frameworks. These frameworks not only shape the policies and practices of DEI but also provide the necessary guidelines to ensure compliance and protect against discrimination. This essay delves into the legal frameworks that shape DEI efforts, highlighting their significance and impact on organizational practices.

The Foundational Laws of DEI

The Civil Rights Act of 1964 (Title VII)

One of the most significant pieces of legislation in the United States that laid the groundwork for DEI is the Civil Rights Act of 1964. Title VII of this act prohibits employment discrimination based on race, color, religion, sex, or national origin. It's a landmark law that has been pivotal in shaping workplace diversity and inclusion policies. Employers with fifteen or more employees are subject to this law, ensuring that a significant portion of the workforce is covered. The Equal Employment Opportunity Commission (EEOC) enforces Title VII, investigating complaints and taking action against discriminatory practices.

The Equal Pay Act of 1963

The Equal Pay Act mandates that men and women receive equal pay for equal work performed in the same workplace. This law addresses gender-based wage disparities and encourages equitable compensation practices. It's a vital component of DEI efforts, emphasizing the importance of equity in financial recognition and career advancement opportunities.

Americans with Disabilities Act (ADA) of 1990

The ADA prohibits discrimination against individuals with disabilities in various areas, including employment, public accommodations, and transportation. Title I of the ADA specifically focuses on employment, requiring employers to provide reasonable accommodations to qualified individuals with disabilities. This law not only fosters inclusion but also promotes accessibility and equal opportunities for all employees.

Age Discrimination in Employment Act (ADEA) of 1967

The ADEA protects employees who are 40 years of age or older from discrimination based on age. This law ensures that older workers are treated fairly and have equal opportunities for hiring, promotion, and other employment benefits. Age diversity is a critical aspect of DEI, and the ADEA reinforces the importance of valuing employees of all ages.

Global Perspectives on DEI Laws

The European Union: General Data Protection Regulation (GDPR)

While GDPR primarily addresses data protection and privacy, it has significant implications for DEI efforts. The regulation mandates that organizations handle personal data, including sensitive information related to race, ethnicity, and health, with utmost care and transparency. This requirement ensures that DEI initiatives involving data collection and analysis are conducted ethically and lawfully.

The United Kingdom: Equality Act 2010

The Equality Act 2010 consolidates various anti-discrimination laws in the UK, covering characteristics such as race, gender, disability, age, religion, and sexual orientation. This comprehensive legislation provides a robust framework for promoting equality and preventing discrimination in employment, education, and other areas. It also introduces the Public Sector Equality Duty, requiring public bodies to consider how their policies and practices impact different protected groups.

Canada: Employment Equity Act

Canada's Employment Equity Act aims to achieve workplace equality by addressing underrepresentation and removing barriers for four designated groups: women, Indigenous peoples, persons with disabilities, and members of visible minorities. Employers are required to analyze their workforce, identify areas of underrepresentation, and develop action plans to address disparities. This proactive approach underscores the importance of strategic planning in DEI efforts.

The Role of Affirmative Action

Affirmative action policies are designed to address historical injustices and promote diversity in education and employment. These policies often involve preferential treatment or targeted recruitment efforts to increase representation of underrepresented groups. While affirmative action remains a contentious issue, it plays a crucial role in advancing DEI goals by actively seeking to level the playing field.

United States: Executive Order 11246

Executive Order 11246, signed by President Lyndon B. Johnson in 1965, mandates affirmative action for federal contractors. It requires them to take proactive steps to ensure equal employment opportunities without regard to race, color, religion, sex, sexual orientation, gender identity, or national origin. The Office of Federal Contract Compliance Programs (OFCCP) enforces this order, conducting compliance evaluations and audits to ensure contractor adherence.

South Africa: Employment Equity Act

South Africa's Employment Equity Act addresses the legacy of apartheid by promoting equitable representation of historically disadvantaged groups in the workforce. The act requires designated employers to implement affirmative action measures, including numerical targets and timeframes, to redress disparities and create a diverse and inclusive workplace.

Challenges and Criticisms

Despite the positive impact of legal frameworks on DEI efforts, challenges and criticisms persist. Critics argue that certain laws, such as affirmative action, may lead to reverse discrimination or tokenism. Moreover, the complexity of navigating multiple legal requirements can pose challenges for organizations, especially those operating in multiple jurisdictions.

Additionally, while laws provide a foundation, they may not always address nuanced issues such as microaggressions, unconscious bias, or intersectionality. Organizations must go beyond legal compliance and foster a culture of genuine inclusion and respect.

Legal frameworks play a pivotal role in shaping DEI efforts, providing the necessary guidelines and protections to promote diversity, equity, and inclusion in various sectors. From foundational laws like the Civil Rights Act to global regulations like GDPR, these legal instruments ensure that organizations uphold ethical and equitable practices.

However, achieving true DEI requires more than legal compliance. It necessitates a commitment to continuous learning, critical self-assessment, and intentional actions that create an environment where everyone can thrive. As society evolves, so too must our understanding and implementation of DEI, ensuring that these principles remain at the heart of our collective progress.

In conclusion, while legal frameworks set the stage for DEI efforts, it is the responsibility of organizations and individuals to build upon this foundation and create a more inclusive and equitable world.

Creating Lasting Change Through Allyship and Advocacy: A DEI Perspective

In today's increasingly global and interconnected world, Diversity, Equity, and Inclusion (DEI) are more than just buzzwords; they are crucial components of a thriving and innovative society. Despite the strides made in promoting DEI, challenges remain. Creating lasting change requires more than policies or training programs; it necessitates active allyship and robust advocacy. This essay explores the pivotal roles that allyship and advocacy play in fostering an inclusive environment, dismantling systemic barriers, and achieving sustainable DEI goals.

Understanding the Concepts

Diversity, Equity, and Inclusion (DEI)

Diversity refers to the presence of differences within a given setting, encompassing various dimensions such as race, gender, age, sexual orientation, religion, and more. **Equity** involves ensuring fair treatment, access, and opportunity for all individuals, while actively working to identify and eliminate barriers that have historically led to disparities. **Inclusion** is the practice of creating environments in which any individual or group can feel welcomed, respected, supported, and valued.

Allyship

Allyship involves individuals from privileged groups using their positions to support and advocate for marginalized communities. Effective allyship requires ongoing self-education, listening, and taking actionable steps to challenge the status quo. It goes beyond passive support and involves a commitment to taking concrete actions aimed at promoting equity and inclusion.

Advocacy

Advocacy is the process of supporting a cause or proposal, including the promotion of policies and practices that advance DEI goals. Advocacy can be personal, such as calling out discriminatory behavior when witnessed, or institutional, such as lobbying for changes in organizational policies or legislation.

The Importance of Allyship and Advocacy in DEI

Fostering Inclusive Environments

Allyship is crucial in creating inclusive environments. When individuals from dominant groups advocate for marginalized communities, it sends a powerful message of solidarity and support. This action helps to establish a culture of inclusion where everyone feels valued. Inclusive environments not only enhance individual well-being but also foster innovation and creativity, as diverse perspectives are actively sought and appreciated.

Dismantling Systemic Barriers

Systemic barriers are deeply rooted in societal structures and institutions, making them challenging to eliminate. Advocacy plays a critical role in identifying and dismantling these barriers. By actively participating in or leading advocacy efforts, allies can help draw attention to inequities and work towards systemic change. This might include policy reforms, educational initiatives, or corporate practices designed to promote equity.

Promoting Sustainable Change

One-time initiatives or events are insufficient for creating lasting DEI change. Sustainable change requires continuous effort and commitment. Both allyship and advocacy contribute to this by maintaining momentum and holding individuals and institutions accountable. Allies who consistently advocate for DEI principles help ensure that these values remain a priority over the long term.

Strategies for Effective Allyship and Advocacy

Continuous Education and Self-Reflection

Effective allies are committed to lifelong learning and self-reflection. This involves understanding the historical and contemporary contexts of marginalized communities and recognizing one's own biases and privileges. Self-education can include reading books, attending workshops, and engaging with diverse perspectives.

Listening and Amplifying Marginalized Voices

Listening to the experiences and perspectives of marginalized individuals is essential. Allies should use their platforms to amplify these voices rather than speaking over them. This can involve sharing content created by marginalized individuals, supporting their initiatives, and ensuring they have opportunities to lead.

Taking Action

True allyship and advocacy require action. This can range from intervening in discriminatory situations to supporting DEI initiatives within organizations. Allies should be prepared to take risks and confront uncomfortable situations to challenge inequities.

Building Coalitions

Collaboration enhances the impact of DEI efforts. Building coalitions with other allies, advocacy groups, and marginalized communities can help create a unified front for change. Collective action amplifies voices and increases the likelihood of achieving meaningful outcomes.

Evaluating and Adapting Strategies

The landscape of DEI is ever-evolving. Effective allies and advocates must regularly evaluate their strategies and adapt as needed. This might involve seeking feedback from marginalized communities, assessing the impact of their actions, and making necessary adjustments.

Challenges and Considerations

Navigating Privilege

One of the challenges of allyship is navigating one's own privilege without centering oneself in the narrative. Allies must balance their role in supporting marginalized communities while ensuring that these communities remain at the forefront of the conversation.

Avoiding Performative Allyship

Performative allyship involves actions that are more about gaining social capital than creating meaningful change. Allies must be wary of this and strive for authentic, sustained engagement.

Addressing Resistance

Resistance to DEI initiatives can come from various quarters. Allies and advocates must be prepared to encounter and address resistance, whether it comes in the form of overt opposition or subtle undermining of efforts.

Creating lasting change through allyship and advocacy is essential for advancing Diversity, Equity, and Inclusion. By fostering inclusive environments, dismantling systemic barriers, and promoting sustainable change, allies and advocates play a crucial role in building a more equitable world. Continuous education, active listening, taking concrete actions, building coalitions, and adapting strategies are key to effective allyship and advocacy. While challenges exist, the commitment to DEI principles can lead to transformative outcomes for individuals and organizations alike. As we strive for a more inclusive future, the roles of allies and advocates will remain indispensable.

Technology and Accessibility in the Context of Diversity, Equity, and Inclusion

Introduction

In today's rapidly evolving digital landscape, technology plays a pivotal role in shaping our society. One critical area where technology can make a significant impact is in promoting Diversity, Equity, and Inclusion (DEI). As businesses, educational institutions, and governments increasingly prioritize DEI initiatives, ensuring that technology is accessible to all is paramount. This essay explores the relationship between technology and accessibility within the DEI context, highlighting the importance of inclusive design, the challenges faced, and potential solutions to create a more equitable digital world.

The Importance of Inclusive Design

Inclusive design is the cornerstone of accessible technology. It involves creating products, services, and environments that are usable by people with the widest range of abilities, ages, and backgrounds. This approach acknowledges that everyone, regardless of their physical or cognitive abilities, should have equal access to technology.

Enhancing User Experience

When technology is designed inclusively, it enhances the user experience for everyone. For instance, features like voice recognition, screen readers, and adjustable font sizes benefit not only individuals with disabilities but also those who may have temporary impairments or simply prefer alternative ways of interacting with technology. By prioritizing inclusivity, designers create solutions that cater to a diverse audience, ultimately improving overall user satisfaction.

Promoting Social Equity

Inclusive technology also promotes social equity by bridging the digital divide. In many parts of the world, marginalized communities face barriers to accessing technology, which can perpetuate social and economic disparities. By designing technology that is accessible to all, we can empower individuals from diverse backgrounds to participate fully in society, access education and employment opportunities, and improve their quality of life.

Challenges in Achieving Accessibility

Despite the clear benefits of inclusive design, there are several challenges that organizations must overcome to achieve true accessibility in technology.

Awareness and Education

One of the primary challenges is a lack of awareness and education about accessibility issues. Many designers and developers are not adequately trained in inclusive design principles, leading to the creation of products that inadvertently exclude certain user groups. To address this, organizations must invest in training programs and resources that educate their workforce about the importance of accessibility and how to implement it in their work.

Limited Resources

Another significant barrier is the limited availability of resources dedicated to accessibility. Small businesses and startups, in particular, may struggle to allocate the necessary funds and time to ensure their products are accessible. Governments and larger organizations can play a crucial role in providing grants, subsidies, and support to help these entities prioritize accessibility.

Rapid Technological Advancements

The rapid pace of technological advancement also poses a challenge. As new technologies emerge, ensuring they are accessible from the outset can be difficult. Continuous monitoring and updates are required to keep up with evolving accessibility standards and to address any issues that may arise. This requires a commitment to ongoing investment and development.

Solutions for Enhancing Accessibility

To overcome these challenges and create a more inclusive digital world, organizations must adopt a proactive approach to accessibility in technology.

Implementing Universal Design Principles

One effective solution is to implement universal design principles, which focus on creating products and environments that are inherently accessible to all, without the need for adaptation or specialized design. By integrating these principles into the design process from the beginning, organizations can ensure that accessibility is a fundamental aspect of their technology.

Leveraging Assistive Technologies

Assistive technologies, such as screen readers, speech recognition software, and adaptive keyboards, play a crucial role in making technology accessible. Organizations should invest in developing and integrating these technologies into their products to support individuals with disabilities. Additionally, partnerships with assistive technology providers can help organizations stay updated on the latest advancements and best practices.

Establishing Accessibility Standards

Establishing and adhering to accessibility standards is essential for creating inclusive technology. Organizations should follow guidelines such as the Web Content Accessibility Guidelines (WCAG) to ensure their digital products meet recognized accessibility criteria. Regular audits and user testing with diverse groups can help identify and address accessibility issues early in the development process.

Fostering a Culture of Inclusion

Creating a culture of inclusion within organizations is critical for sustaining accessibility efforts. This involves promoting diversity within teams, encouraging open dialogue about accessibility challenges, and recognizing and rewarding efforts to improve inclusivity. Leadership should prioritize accessibility as a core value, setting an example for the entire organization.

In the context of Diversity, Equity, and Inclusion, technology has the potential to be a powerful equalizer, providing opportunities and improving the quality of life for individuals from all walks of life. However, achieving true accessibility requires a concerted effort from organizations, designers, developers, and policymakers. By embracing inclusive design principles, addressing challenges head-on, and fostering a culture of inclusion, we can create a digital world that is accessible to all, ensuring that no one is left behind in the technological revolution.

Global Perspectives on Diversity, Equity, and Inclusion (DEI)

Diversity, Equity, and Inclusion (DEI) have become central themes in the global discourse on workplace culture, societal progression, and human rights. However, the interpretation and implementation of DEI principles vary significantly across different regions and cultures. This article aims to explore these global perspectives, highlighting the commonalities and unique approaches that shape our collective understanding of DEI.

The United States: A Legacy of Advocacy

In the United States, the DEI movement is heavily rooted in its history of civil rights activism. The U.S. has long been a melting pot of cultures, and the push for diversity and inclusion has been driven by a need to address historical injustices, such as slavery and segregation.

Key Focus Areas:

- **Racial and Ethnic Diversity**: Efforts include affirmative action policies and diversity quotas in education and employment.

- **Gender Equity**: The #MeToo movement has profoundly impacted workplace policies, leading to stricter anti-harassment regulations.

- **LGBTQ+ Rights**: Legal advancements, like the legalization of same-sex marriage, illustrate progress, but discrimination remains an issue.

Challenges:

- **Systemic Racism**: Despite significant strides, systemic racism continues to impact various sectors, including criminal justice, healthcare, and education.

- **Political Polarization**: DEI initiatives often become politicized, leading to resistance and backlash in certain areas.

Europe: A Mixed Bag of Approaches

Europe presents a diverse landscape of DEI practices, largely influenced by its complex history and current political climate.

Western Europe:

Countries like the United Kingdom, Germany, and France have robust DEI frameworks, emphasizing gender equity, anti-discrimination laws, and support for immigrants.

- **Gender Quotas**: Many Western European countries have implemented gender quotas in corporate boards and political offices.

- **Anti-Discrimination Legislation**: Comprehensive laws protect against discrimination based on race, gender, religion, and sexual orientation.

Eastern Europe:

In contrast, Eastern European countries are relatively new to the DEI discourse, grappling with challenges such as nationalism and historical legacies of homogeneity.

- **Cultural Homogeneity**: Countries like Poland and Hungary have less diverse populations, making the implementation of DEI initiatives more challenging.

- **LGBTQ+ Rights**: LGBTQ+ rights are often a contentious issue, with some countries adopting anti-LGBTQ+ policies.

Challenges:

- **Economic Disparities**: Economic inequalities between Western and Eastern Europe impact the prioritization and implementation of DEI initiatives.

- **Migratory Pressures**: The refugee crisis has strained resources and heightened xenophobic sentiments in some regions.

Asia: Balancing Tradition and Modernity

Asia's approach to DEI is shaped by its vast cultural diversity and rapid economic development. Countries in this region are navigating the balance between traditional values and modern DEI principles.

Japan and South Korea:

These nations have traditionally homogenous societies but are increasingly embracing DEI due to globalization and demographic challenges.

- **Gender Equity**: Initiatives like "Womenomics" in Japan aim to increase female workforce participation.

- **Workplace Inclusion**: Efforts are underway to create more inclusive workplaces for people with disabilities.

India:

India's DEI landscape is complex, influenced by its caste system, religious diversity, and economic disparities.

- **Caste-Based Reservations**: Affirmative action policies aim to uplift historically marginalized communities.

- **Religious Diversity**: Efforts to promote interfaith harmony are crucial in a multi-religious society.

Challenges:

- **Cultural Norms**: Traditional gender roles and societal norms can impede DEI progress.

- **Economic Inequality**: Stark economic disparities pose significant challenges to achieving equity.

Africa: A Continent of Contrasts

Africa's DEI narrative is deeply intertwined with its colonial history, ethnic diversity, and varying levels of economic development.

South Africa:

South Africa is a leader in DEI efforts on the continent, driven by its history of apartheid and the subsequent push for racial reconciliation.

- **Black Economic Empowerment (BEE)**: Policies aim to redress the economic inequalities created by apartheid.

- **Gender Equity**: There are strong legal frameworks for gender equality, although implementation remains inconsistent.

Other African Nations:

DEI efforts vary widely, influenced by local contexts and priorities.

- **Ethnic Diversity**: Countries like Nigeria and Kenya grapple with ethnic diversity, focusing on ethnic harmony and inclusive governance.

- **Economic Inclusion**: Efforts to include marginalized communities in economic activities are ongoing.

Challenges:

- **Political Instability**: Political unrest and corruption can hinder DEI initiatives.

- **Resource Constraints**: Limited resources often mean that DEI is not a top priority.

A Global Imperative

While the approaches to DEI differ across the globe, the underlying principles of promoting diversity, ensuring equity, and fostering inclusion remain universal. As we continue to navigate complex social landscapes, it is crucial to learn from each other's experiences and collaborate on building a more inclusive world.

For organizations looking to integrate DEI principles, understanding these global perspectives can provide valuable insights and drive impactful actions. Together, we can create environments where everyone has the opportunity to thrive, regardless of their background.

The Future of DEI: Trends, Predictions, and Next Steps

Diversity, Equity, and Inclusion (DEI) have evolved from being buzzwords to critical components of progressive organizational cultures. As we move further into the 21st century, the importance of DEI is not only recognized but also actively pursued by forward-thinking organizations. This essay explores the future of DEI, examining current trends, making predictions for the coming years, and suggesting actionable next steps for organizations committed to fostering an inclusive and equitable environment.

Current Trends in DEI

1. Data-Driven DEI Initiatives

Organizations are increasingly relying on data to drive their DEI initiatives. By leveraging data analytics, companies can identify disparities, monitor progress, and measure the impact of their DEI strategies. This trend towards a data-driven approach allows organizations to be more transparent and accountable in their DEI efforts.

2. Focus on Intersectionality

Intersectionality, a term coined by Kimberlé Crenshaw, refers to the interconnected nature of social categorizations such as race, gender, and class, which can create overlapping systems of discrimination or disadvantage. Recognizing the complexity of individual identities, organizations are adopting intersectional approaches to DEI, ensuring that policies and practices are inclusive of all aspects of an individual's identity.

3. Inclusive Leadership

Inclusive leadership is becoming a key focus area for organizations. This involves training leaders to recognize their biases, understand the value of diverse perspectives, and create environments where all employees feel valued and included. Leadership development programs now often include DEI components to ensure that inclusivity is embedded at all levels of the organization.

4. Remote Work and DEI

The shift to remote work, accelerated by the COVID-19 pandemic, has had significant implications for DEI. While remote work can offer flexibility and inclusivity, it also presents challenges such as digital divide and isolation. Organizations are working to address these challenges by implementing policies that promote digital inclusion and ensure that remote workers have equal access to opportunities.

5. Employee Resource Groups (ERGs)

Employee Resource Groups (ERGs) have become vital in fostering an inclusive culture within organizations. These groups provide a platform for employees to connect, share experiences, and advocate for change. ERGs also play a crucial role in informing organizational DEI strategies and initiatives.

Predictions for the Future of DEI

1. AI and DEI

Artificial Intelligence (AI) will play a significant role in shaping the future of DEI. AI can be used to analyze large datasets, identify trends, and automate processes to reduce bias in hiring, promotions, and performance evaluations. However, organizations must be cautious and ensure that AI systems are designed and implemented in ways that do not reinforce existing biases.

2. Global DEI Standards

As globalization continues to connect markets and cultures, there will be a push towards establishing global DEI standards. Internationally recognized frameworks and guidelines will help organizations implement consistent and effective DEI practices across different regions and cultures.

3. Mental Health and DEI

The intersection of mental health and DEI will gain more attention. Organizations will recognize the importance of creating inclusive environments that support mental well-being. This will involve addressing issues such as workplace stress, discrimination, and providing resources for mental health support.

4. Transparency and Accountability

Stakeholders, including employees, customers, and investors, will demand greater transparency and accountability from organizations regarding their DEI efforts. Companies will need to publicly report on their DEI goals, progress, and outcomes. This will drive organizations to be more proactive in their DEI initiatives and adopt best practices.

5. Customization of DEI Strategies

One-size-fits-all approaches to DEI will become obsolete. Organizations will increasingly tailor their DEI strategies to address the unique needs and challenges of their workforce. This will involve engaging employees in the development of DEI initiatives and continuously evolving strategies based on feedback and outcomes.

Next Steps for Organizations Committed to DEI

1. Conduct a DEI Audit

A thorough DEI audit is the first step in understanding an organization's current state of diversity, equity, and inclusion. This involves collecting and analyzing data on workforce demographics, policies, practices, and employee experiences. The insights gained from the audit will inform the development of targeted DEI initiatives.

2. Set Clear and Measurable Goals

Organizations should establish clear and measurable DEI goals that align with their overall business objectives. These goals should be specific, achievable, and time-bound. Examples include increasing the representation of underrepresented groups in leadership positions or improving employee engagement and satisfaction scores.

3. Invest in DEI Training and Education

Continuous education and training are essential for fostering an inclusive culture. Organizations should invest in comprehensive DEI training programs that cover topics such as unconscious bias, cultural competency, and inclusive leadership. These programs should be mandatory for all employees, including leadership.

4. Empower Employee Resource Groups (ERGs)

ERGs should be empowered with the resources and support they need to thrive. This includes providing funding, executive sponsorship, and opportunities for ERG leaders to contribute to organizational decision-making. ERGs can serve as valuable partners in driving DEI initiatives and creating a sense of belonging.

5. Implement Inclusive Policies and Practices

Organizations must review and update their policies and practices to ensure they are inclusive and equitable. This includes areas such as recruitment, performance evaluations, promotions, and benefits. Policies should be designed to eliminate bias and create equal opportunities for all employees.

6. Leverage Technology for DEI

Technology can be a powerful tool in advancing DEI efforts. Organizations should leverage AI and data analytics to identify and address disparities, automate processes, and track progress. Additionally, technology can facilitate remote work and create inclusive virtual environments for employees.

7. Foster an Inclusive Culture

Building an inclusive culture requires ongoing effort and commitment from all levels of the organization. This involves creating a safe space for open dialogue, encouraging diverse perspectives, and recognizing and celebrating diversity. Leadership plays a crucial role in modeling inclusive behavior and setting the tone for the organization.

8. Engage with External Partners

Organizations can benefit from engaging with external partners such as DEI consultants, industry associations, and community organizations. These partnerships can provide valuable insights, resources, and support for DEI initiatives. Additionally, collaborating with external partners can help organizations stay informed about best practices and emerging trends in DEI.

9. Monitor and Evaluate Progress

Regular monitoring and evaluation are essential to ensure the effectiveness of DEI initiatives. Organizations should establish metrics and key performance indicators (KPIs) to track progress towards DEI goals. This includes conducting regular surveys, focus groups, and audits to gather feedback and assess the impact of DEI efforts.

10. Publicly Report on DEI Efforts

Transparency is key to building trust and accountability. Organizations should publicly report on their DEI goals, progress, and outcomes. This can be done through annual reports, sustainability reports, or dedicated DEI reports. Public reporting demonstrates a commitment to DEI and allows stakeholders to hold the organization accountable.

The future of DEI is promising, with organizations increasingly recognizing the value of diversity, equity, and inclusion. By embracing current trends, anticipating future developments, and taking actionable steps, organizations can create inclusive environments that drive innovation, engagement, and success. As we move forward, it is essential for organizations to remain committed to continuous improvement and to adapt their DEI strategies to meet the evolving needs of their workforce and society. Through collaborative efforts and a genuine commitment to DEI, we can build a more equitable and inclusive future for all.

DEI: A Caribbean Perspective

Diversity, Equity, and Inclusion (DEI) have become focal points in discussions about social development and organizational culture globally. In the Caribbean Region, a mosaic of cultures, languages, and ethnic backgrounds presents a unique landscape for DEI initiatives. Historically, the Caribbean has been a melting pot of diverse influences due to colonization, slavery, and migration. This essay explores the progress of DEI in the Caribbean, examining key sectors such as education, employment, and governance, while highlighting challenges and potential pathways for further advancement.

Historical Context

Colonial Legacy and Its Impact

The Caribbean's colonial past has significantly influenced its current social and economic structures. Colonizers from Europe brought enslaved Africans and indentured laborers from Asia, creating a multi-ethnic society marked by deep social stratification and racial hierarchies. These historical inequities have left a lasting legacy that continues to impact DEI efforts today.

Independence and Nation-Building

With the wave of independence movements in the mid-20th century, many Caribbean nations began the process of nation-building. These efforts focused on fostering national unity while grappling with the complex task of addressing historical injustices and promoting social equity. Independence brought a renewed sense of identity and purpose, but the remnants of colonial-era discrimination persisted, necessitating focused DEI initiatives.

Education Sector

Access to Education

Significant strides have been made in increasing access to education across the Caribbean. Governments have implemented policies to ensure that primary and secondary education is accessible to all children, regardless of their background. For instance, countries like Barbados and Trinidad and Tobago boast high literacy rates and near-universal primary school enrollment. However, disparities still exist, particularly in rural areas and among marginalized communities.

Curriculum Reform

Curriculum reform has been a critical component of DEI progress in the education sector. Efforts have been made to decolonize the curriculum, incorporating more content that reflects the diverse histories and cultures of the Caribbean. This includes teaching indigenous histories, African heritage, and the contributions of various ethnic groups to Caribbean society. Such reforms aim to create a more inclusive educational environment that respects and celebrates diversity.

Higher Education and Representation

Higher education institutions have also been pivotal in advancing DEI. Universities across the region have established research centers and programs focused on social justice, equality, and inclusion. Initiatives aimed at increasing the representation of underrepresented groups in academia have seen some success, though challenges remain in ensuring equitable access to tertiary education.

Employment Sector

Workforce Diversity

The Caribbean's workforce is inherently diverse due to its multicultural population. However, achieving true equity and inclusion within the workplace remains a work in progress. Efforts to promote workforce diversity have included affirmative action policies and diversity training programs. Companies are increasingly recognizing the value of diverse teams in fostering innovation and driving business success.

Gender Equity

Gender equity has been a significant focus area within the Caribbean employment sector. Women have made substantial gains in workforce participation and leadership roles. For instance, the Caribbean has seen a rise in female entrepreneurs and women holding executive positions in both the public and private sectors. Legislative measures, such as gender quotas and equal pay laws, have been instrumental in promoting gender equity.

Addressing Racial and Ethnic Disparities

Despite progress, racial and ethnic disparities persist in the Caribbean workforce. Afro-Caribbean and indigenous communities often face higher unemployment rates and limited access to high-paying jobs. Addressing these disparities requires targeted interventions, including mentorship programs, skills training, and anti-discrimination policies.

Governance and Political Representation

Inclusive Governance

Inclusive governance is crucial for ensuring that DEI principles are embedded in national policies and practices. Caribbean nations have made efforts to promote inclusive governance by implementing constitutional reforms and establishing human rights commissions. These bodies work to protect the rights of marginalized groups and hold governments accountable for DEI commitments.

Political Representation

Political representation of diverse groups has improved over the years, with more women and ethnic minorities holding political office. Countries like Jamaica and Trinidad and Tobago have seen women elected to high-ranking positions, including prime ministerial roles. However, there is still room for improvement in ensuring that political leadership reflects the full spectrum of Caribbean diversity.

Civil Society and Advocacy

Civil society organizations play a vital role in advancing DEI in the Caribbean. Advocacy groups, non-governmental organizations, and grassroots movements work tirelessly to raise awareness, lobby for policy changes, and support marginalized communities. These organizations are instrumental in driving social change and holding authorities accountable.

Challenges and Barriers

Socio-Economic Inequities

One of the significant challenges to DEI progress in the Caribbean is the persistence of socio-economic inequities. Poverty, limited access to quality education, and lack of economic opportunities disproportionately affect marginalized communities. Addressing these root causes is essential for creating a more equitable society.

Cultural Attitudes and Stereotypes

Cultural attitudes and stereotypes can also hinder DEI efforts. Deep-seated prejudices and biases against certain groups, including LGBTQ+ individuals and people with disabilities, create barriers to inclusion. Changing these cultural attitudes requires comprehensive public education campaigns and strong legal protections against discrimination.

Institutional Resistance

Institutional resistance to DEI initiatives can slow progress. Some organizations and individuals may be reluctant to change long-standing practices or may not see the value in prioritizing DEI. Overcoming this resistance requires strong leadership, clear communication of the benefits of DEI, and sustained commitment to change.

Pathways for Further Advancement

Strengthening Legal Frameworks

Strengthening legal frameworks is critical for advancing DEI in the Caribbean. Governments must enact and enforce robust anti-discrimination laws, ensuring that all individuals are protected from bias and prejudice. Additionally, policies promoting affirmative action and equal opportunity can help level the playing field.

Enhancing Education and Awareness

Education and awareness are powerful tools for driving DEI progress. Schools and universities should continue to decolonize curricula and promote inclusive education. Public awareness campaigns can challenge stereotypes and promote positive attitudes towards diversity. Building a culture of inclusion starts with changing hearts and minds.

Fostering Inclusive Workplaces

Creating truly inclusive workplaces requires ongoing effort and commitment. Organizations should implement comprehensive diversity and inclusion strategies, including regular training, mentorship programs, and transparent hiring practices. Promoting a culture of inclusion benefits not only employees but also the organization as a whole.

Supporting Grassroots Movements

Grassroots movements and civil society organizations are essential drivers of DEI progress. Supporting these groups through funding, capacity-building, and collaboration can amplify their impact. Governments and businesses should partner with civil society to create a united front for DEI.

Leveraging Technology and Innovation

Technology and innovation offer new opportunities for advancing DEI. Digital platforms can facilitate access to education, employment, and services for marginalized communities. AI and data analytics can help identify and address disparities. Leveraging technology enables more effective and scalable DEI initiatives.

The Caribbean has made significant strides in advancing diversity, equity, and inclusion across various sectors. However, challenges remain, and the path to true equity is ongoing. By strengthening legal frameworks, enhancing education and awareness, fostering inclusive workplaces, supporting grassroots movements, and leveraging technology, the Caribbean can continue to build a more just and inclusive society.

The progress of DEI in the Caribbean is a testament to the region's resilience and commitment to social justice. As the Caribbean navigates its unique challenges and opportunities, it serves as a model for other regions striving to create a more equitable world. The road ahead may be long, but with sustained effort and collaboration, the vision of a truly inclusive Caribbean is within reach.

References

1. "Why diversity and inclusion matter - McKinsey & Company". www.mckinsey.com, https://www.mckinsey.com/business-functions/organization/our-insights/why-diversity-and-inclusion-matter. Accessed 22 May 2021.

2. Mankin, A., & Garton, E. (2020). The diversity dividend: How organizations can financially benefit from diversity and inclusion efforts. Harvard Business Review Digital Articles, 1-8.

3. "The business case for diversity". Catalyst, https://www.catalyst.org

Resources

- **Society for Human Resource Management (SHRM)**

- **Diversity Inc. Best Practices**

- **Human Rights Campaign Corporate Equality Index**

9 789768 341440